beautiful napkins

beautiful napkins

stylish ideas for your table

margaret caselton

photography by david loftus

RUNNING PRESS
Philadelphia • London

Designer **Paul Tilby**

Senior Editor **Sian Parkhouse**

Production **Patricia Harrington**

Publishing Director **Anne Ryland**

Stylist **Margaret Caselton**

Library of Congress Cataloging-in-
Publication number 98-66881

ISBN 0-7624-0440-X

Printed and bound in China

This edition published in the
United States in 1999 by
Running Press Book Publishers
125 South Twenty-second Street
Philadelphia, Pennsylvania
19103-4399

Visit us on the web!
www.runningpress.com

contents

introduction

As practical and useful an object as anything else on the table, the napkin can also be the most decorative element. No table setting is complete without this vital ingredient. Tableware does not have to match—table linens can be brightly colored, soft, pastel, checks, stripes, or if you want, for special occasions you can use a traditional large damask for effect and formality. It is hoped that the ideas in this book will assist, encourage, and give confidence to anyone wanting to create an inviting table setting.

napkins in history

The history of the napkin is a long and interesting one. Indeed, one anonymous French researcher has taken the subject so seriously that he or she refers to the 1960s and '70s as the era of "emancipation"— of the napkin and table setting rather than social constraints!

There is without doubt an emancipation in the rigors of table etiquette from earlier this century when only "double damask" would do and Emily Post, author of *Etiquette: The Blue Book of Social Usage*, pronounced that "napkins should never . . . . be put on the side, because it looks as though you are showing off the beauty of your place plate" or "very fancy foldings are not in good taste" and every household dutifully obeyed. Meal times could not have been much fun when everyone was spending their time checking that every affectation of manners was being slavishly obeyed.

Today there are no ridiculous rules—only those of consideration and courtesy. At private dinner parties, the trend is toward creating a good ambience with the settings and lighting. The emphasis is on making guests feel welcome and comfortable by creating a convivial atmosphere. This can be helped with a well-planned table setting. Placecards, fun foldings of napkins, fresh flowers and herbs tucked into napkins, and personalized napkin rings all create talking points, make guests feel you have taken care, help the party get started, and above all make people feel a fine feast is about to take place.

above A traditional double damask napkin in a silver napkin indicates a formal dinner setting. In the Middle Ages the size of napkin would have indicated the rank of the guest.

opposite Starched damask napkins are stacked in preparation for a dinner. In earlier times, when large households employed a team of staff, there were servants whose exclusive job it was to care for the linen.

Contemporary etiquette, according to Drusilla Beyfus in *Modern Manners*, suggests that napkins can either be laid in the center of a place setting or alternatively placed on the side plate. But the only golden rule, she says, is "whatever its design, a napkin should always look and feel freshly laundered".

It is believed the ancient Romans introduced napkins, and curiously these were of bright colors. Two napkins were used: one large napkin was tied around the neck, and slaves would pour perfumed water over the guests' hands and dry them with a second napkin. It was during the Middle Ages that table linen became fashionable, and by the 16th century most of the wealthier households would lay tables. People at that time ate with their fingers and a knife, and either wiped their hands on the tablecloth or on their bread. Therefore the tablecloth

was changed several times during the meal; sometimes two or three cloths were laid one over the other. (In some restaurants a change of cloth during the meal is still a custom.) Another method was to lay a border or "cover" of linen over the edge of the table, which is the origin of the restaurant "cover" charge.

The size of napkin a guest brought to a meal would signify his wealth. Therefore the larger the napkin, the wealthier the guest. Servants would tie the napkin around the neck like a bib, and if the napkin was of an "economic" size, it was said that they "could just make ends meet." Napkins belonging to the "seigneur" were large and luxurious, and often magnificently embroidered with fringed borders. They were draped over the diner's arm—something which we see in formal restaurants and which could have developed from this ancient custom.

opposite This formal place setting has a white damask napkin and flatware for two courses. Napkins are usually placed on top of the dinner plate or, alternatively, on the left-hand side of the setting.

right An informal lunch or family setting requires only enough flatware for one course—in this instance, the knife and fork may be placed together on top of the napkin on the right-hand side of the diner's plate.

From earliest times napkins were also used to cover food to protect it from poisoning as it passed from the kitchen to the table (at the Court of Versailles outside Paris this was said to be a distance of a quarter of a mile, so there was plenty of opportunity for anyone with nefarious purposes to interfere with the food). In each of his residences, the French king had a special officer to take care of his napkins—the *garde-nappe*. All household linens were perfumed with lavender and roses, and kept in locked wooden chests or leather coffers.

above In formal restaurants or dinners, a white napkin is often placed over the waiter's arm, a tradition that its origins in the Middle Ages.

right Napkins are sometimes used to place around the neck of a wine bottle to prevent drips or splashing when wine is poured, and to soak up condensation.

this page The napkin is shaken out and then laid on the lap when the diner is seated. This is done either by the diner or, on formal occasions, by the waiter in attendance.

Napkins, too, follow the dictates of fashion. In the times of ruffs and large lace collars—particularly for men—napkins were, of necessity, enormous – more than a yard square in order to cover these elaborate accessories. But as fashions changed, so did the style of napkin, and by the early 19th century the way in which it was used became a subject of scrutiny. The French still sometimes use the napkin as a bib, but this practice is not common in the English-speaking world, and it may look as though the diner has an appetite commensurate with the size of his napkin, which could look very greedy! Napkins are usually unfolded and put on your lap as soon as you sit down; in some restaurants the waiter will do it for you. At the end of the meal a napkin is left crumpled on the table and not folded again—unless of course it is a family meal and each member has their own napkin ring and the napkin is to be re-used. Nowadays, we only use napkins to dab our mouths or wipe our hands, but its original employment was much more necessary. With the introduction of the fork, napkins became less soiled during the meal.

In the 17th century, particularly in France, there was a tremendous vogue for folded napkins. One can imagine the drama and theater of special celebrations when napkins were folded into the shapes of animals, butterflies, chickens with eggs, fruit, birds, and many other complex shapes. Napkin folding was then a profession in itself, and the "Napkin Folder" was employed by wealthy households to arrive the day before and create these displays. Banquets and feasts must have been quite amazing and lasted for many hours. There was a great sense of occasion, and it is perhaps this sense of theater and excitement we can re-create on our own table with the plethora of materials and decorations we have at our disposal.

left A napkin is always left crumpled on the table after a meal to indicate that it is ready to be laundered, unless it is a family occasion and each family member has a personal ring to keep and identify their napkin for several meals.

classic napkins

Dining etiquette may have relaxed considerably in recent years, but it is still gratifying on special occasions to go to town on your table settings and use the most elegant and high-quality table linens to complement your best china, silverware, and crystal.

sizes and types of napkin

It has been traditional since the 17th century for large white napkins to be used on formal occasions. Table linen, just like clothes, has its changing fashions, and today we enjoy a wonderful choice of napkins, from the formal to the purely decorative. There is a napkin for every type of function, from banquets, weddings, luncheons, and afternoon tea and cocktail parties, to casual gatherings of friends and family.

The type of napkin usually denotes the level of formality. The most popular style is a crisply starched white or cream damask or plain-woven linen napkin for luncheon and dinner occasions. However, pale pink or mint green is often used as an acceptable alternative for celebrations such as "coming of age," engagement, or an anniversary.

There are only very general rules as to the correct size of a napkin. In France and other parts of Europe, they are generous—approximately a yard or more square, especially those handmade in the late 19th century from handloom linens. These often featured eleborate embroidered initials. In England, one of the finest dinner napkins is the "double damask." Damask is a firm self-patterned fabric made on a jacquard loom. Traditionally made of silk from Damascus, it can now be made from cotton, silk, wool or a combination of fibers. The richly figurative design is produced by the contrast of a sateen weft against a satin warp. On a double damask the pattern is represented on both sides of the napkin. Linen is preferable to cotton since it is resistant to sunlight, and is stronger, cooler, absorbs moisture more readily, dries more quickly, has more luster, and soils less quickly than cotton.

opposite Various napkin sizes: cocktail, tea, lunch, dinner, and traditional early 20th-century French.
left A napkin is laid on a plate for a formal dinner.
above right A "double damask" dinner napkin is most luxurious.

monogramming

Monogramming is the classic form of ornamentation on napkins; a monogram stitched in white thread on white fabric can be so perfect it almost looks embossed. Adding an embroidered initial is a good way to personalize a napkin for a gift.

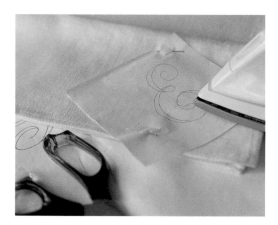

one Make a plain napkin by hemming around a large square of fine linen. Select the letter you want from the iron-on transfers and position it in one corner, making sure

it lines up exactly with the corner. Pin it in place and then press with a hot iron to transfer the image onto the linen.

two Using all strands, use embroidery floss to fill in the outline of the letter in satin stitch: make small parallel lines very close together so no fabric shows through, and work from one end of the letter to another.

lift flap ▶

right A crisply starched, freshly laundered classic white linen napkin is an indispensible adornment to your table. It will add gravitas and style to any any dining experience.

Traditional dinner napkins vary in size from 30 inches square down to 20 inches. Anything smaller than this should really be used for luncheon or a late supper. Luncheon napkins are more decorative and less formal than those used for dinner. Many feature embellishments such as embroidery in one corner, a woven or printed border pattern, faggotting or drawn thread work, an all-over pattern such as stripes and checks, or a solid color.

The style of the table setting can be used as a guide to the formality or spirit of the occasion. Afternoon tea napkins are approximately 8 to 10 inches square, and can, but do not have to be, laid on the lap. They are provided to wipe the mouth and fingers. In the 19th and early 20th century, when morning coffee or afternoon tea was still a pertinent social occasion, napkins were often exquisitely embroidered.

Cocktail or finger napkins are made from less sturdy, often flimsy, fashionable fabric. There are many pretty and dainty varieties of such napkins, made from lace, organza, and organdy to fine cotton voile. Cocktail napkins are from 6 inches square down to handkerchief size and are vital for wiping the hands after canapés or finger food. On a formal occasion the waiter will carry a small stack of small napkins which are proffered once you have eaten and then discarded on a tray offered for the purpose.

right Champagne and strawberries are perfect for a summer's day, and fine Swiss linen scalloped-edged and embroidered cocktail napkins are a charming accompaniment. Settings can be enhanced by linking the napkin decoration to that on the china or glassware. Here the curves on the napkin echo the more graphic curves on the Christian Lacroix teaplate.

opposite An inviting afternoon tea tray is set with a white tray cloth and fine linen and organza appliquéd napkins.

Whole sets of fine table linen bought new in department stores can be a major investment, which is why they are a perennial and very sensible inclusion on many wedding lists! However, if you are not in a position to plan your nuptials to your material advantage, or you haven't been lucky enough to inherit your grandmother's vintage table linen, there are other ways of acquiring a set.

Country fairs and bric-à-brac shops are a rich source for table linens. It is unusual to come across a complete set all together, but don't reject single napkins. Neutral colors such as white or ivory can be mixed together. Or buy a set of relatively inexpensive plain-weave white linen napkins and combine them with more elaborate damasks and embroidered napkins as you acquire them.

above left This classic single setting demonstrates the basic arrangement of a folded damask napkin just overlapping the top and bottom of the dinner plate. Dinner napkins may look meager in size if they do not cover the plate and show a double fold. A napkin should always be generous enough to cover the guest's lap comfortably.

below left A detail of a double damask napkin shows the traditional damask rose pattern.

opposite After large functions such as a wedding and in restaurants, it is common practice to lay a tablecoth or large napkin on the floor and throw used napkins into it. These are then grouped together in bunches and tied up in a "mother" napkin in sets of ten or more to await pick-up by the laundry service.

themes

There are a plethora of ways in which to create a lively tablescape, but more than any other element, it is napkins that add the finishing touch. Formal or informal, al fresco or festive—the type, color, fabric, and decoration of a napkin can really set off the table, whatever the occasion. There are many innovative ideas and themes to choose from, from checks and stripes to damasks and florals.

far left A set of bright linen napkins decorated with faggotted hems creates a kaleidoscope of color on a table top.

left Bold contrasting primary-colored borders add extra interest to plain white napkins.

solid colors

Collections of plain napkins make a stunning table setting, especially when offset by plain white china. Often described as "harlequin" sets, they can be of different colors and assorted textiles, but can look harmonious when they are similar in size, so they can be folded in the same way on each plate.

One method is to collect in color tones—from the primary colors of blue, red, and yellow, which look remarkable combined with bold colors such as orange, green, purple, turquoise, and even black, to the paler sherbert shades of pistachio, lilac, pink, primrose, and baby blue. It is amusing to alternate with plain white if you have only a few colored napkins. Household linen departments usually carry sets of plain napkins, or it is simple to make your own by hemming around a square of solid-colored cotton dress fabric.

left and below left An informal but chic luncheon setting: the juxtaposition of red (with a tonal border of orange) set against a ribbed cotton black table mat and white plate creates a bold contemporary mood.

opposite and inset Early summer supper for two: the combination of sharp red and orange on napkin and cloth is innovative and appealing.

It is important when using brightly colored table linen to decide your menu. The sharp tones of an orange and pale silver bowl complement the young green of crisp lettuce. However, if your menu were to include red meat, it would work better with paler linens.

Color combinations are fun to work on. If you do not already have one, obtain a color wheel that shows complementary colors and the tones and hues derived from them, or use a paint color chart. Opposites and vibrant, sometimes clashing, colors such as orange and shocking pink also work well together for the right occasion.

opposite and above A *coupe rouge* of red fruit is set upon a pale pink damask napkin placed diamond-shape on a white tablecloth.

below These fine handmade tea napkins in pale green have a white castellated scalloped edge.

Pale pink and green is a well-recognized combination of colors that harmonize well. They always create a light, relaxed mood and atmosphere, and are the perfect background for a bunch of soft summer roses, daisies, or meadow flowers. Pastel colors suggest a traditional table setting so they provide the perfect opportunity to bring out your most decorative tableware. Ornate silverware and treasured pieces such as elegant cake stands or a gilt-edged tea set will be complemented gracefully by delicately toned napkins. Translucent or frosted glass and your finest bone china are also appropriate choices for this type of setting.

Spring and summer with its variety of flowers and fruits is a perfect time to experiment with romantic table settings and soft colors. Paler colors can be used to great effect as a foil for the rich colors of vibrant green salads and bright summer berries. Outdoor dining is one of the most indulgent pleasures of the summer, and softer shades of table linen will look perfect in the dappled sunlight of a late summer's afternoon.

left Shades of forest and herb green napkins set upon white plates and a polished steel table top create a subtle link of natural colors. There are myriad shades of each color and a coordinated collection brings a harmony of color to the table. Again a plain napkin is always thrown into relief by white underplates, but when shades are very close, patterns can work very effectively.

right Table mats and napkins with pretty plain borders make a minimal table setting attractive. The combinations of different colors in close proximity is important, and it is worth working these out first for best results. The choice of china, flatware and glassware should also be simple when there are a lot of colors at work.

There is an abundance of plain colors in tableware. Plates can be mixed harlequin style as effectively as napkins can. A colored napkin placed between two colored plates creates variety—or two sets of tableware can be mixed with a spectrum of colored napkins.

Contemporary china has moved beyond the traditional dinner set and incorporates dishes and colors used in other cultures. Some of this tableware features unusual

right Two equally strong colors can work together to great effect.

below A vibrant oriental setting with a fuschia and red organdy napkin and clashing red chopsticks is offset by a bowl in contemporary matte black.

shapes, such as deep bowls and square underplates, and different finishes, such as smooth matte or crackle glazes, are a perfect foil for plain solid colors. Contemporary Western designs in china and linens can combine perfectly with traditional Eastern-style table settings.

above An unusual setting of purple, pale silver, and eggplant is decorated with a sprig of basil that can be eaten between courses to cleanse the palette.

Even the most ad hoc of dining occasions, such as a casual lunch for two friends, can be improved by the judicious use of tableware. Here, an almost accidental combination of glassware, oriental china, and bistro flatware is all brought together by the fanned topping of the green two-tone napkin. A haphazard mixture of textures and similar shades combines to bring out the maximum effect of green tonal variations.

Regardless of occasion, it can be an interesting exercise to group together tabletop pieces in varied color tones, and see what happens. Pale-toned but colorful napkins are a good fallback when unexpected guests arrive, because they can combine easily with most tableware and will enliven even the most homey setting.

spring greens

above   A two-tone napkin is fanned out to draw attention to its unusual dual coloring.

opposite and right   The casual knot in the napkin adds a decorative detail to a light lunch, Italian style. Although the meal is simply a midday snack, the occasion and setting are enhanced by the use of fun napkins and stylish plates and flatware.

nothin' but the blues

A collection of different tones and textures themed around one color is ideal for big parties as well as everyday occasions. Blue is ideal for this treatment because the spectrum is vast: from violet to indigo through to sky blue. *Isatis tinctoria*, or woad, was the traditional dye in Europe until indigo was introduced. Natural indigo dye is used in many cultures, particularly Japan, and there are some lovely dyed cloths, ancient and modern, to be found.

Soft denim, cheerful cotton checks, stripes, plain borders, and patterned blues are all useful. White china is a good foil for blue, and, depending on the shades, can be the ideal companion for traditional blue and white china. However, blue checked and blue-rimmed dishes work best.

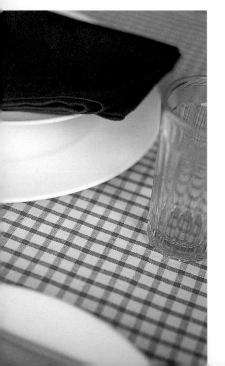

lift flap ▶

white on white

The most traditional napkins for formal occasions are white damask or linen—freshly laundered, crisply starched, and set on a perfectly folded tablecloth with a sharp crease that runs vertically along the center of the table. Once table linens were kept in linen presses in order to keep the folds as sharp as possible.

The formal white napkin has a long history, and when used as covers in past times, it was an important sign that they were clean and undefiled. White napkins for our most auspicious occasions should be generous—the bigger the better—and can, because of their crispness, be folded to augment the full effect of a wonderfully inviting tablescape gleaming with glass, silver, and linen.

left   A small army of damask napkins, folded into "Bishop's Miters", are ready to be set on plates for a formal banquet.

this page Soft table linen with decorative fringed edges nestles under a craftsman potter's bowl and saucer. The theme of white on white unifies the setting and means the rough texture of handmade pottery can sit comfortably with soft linen.

opposite above Again the combination of textures—smooth contemporary tableware, sheer organza and fine-weave linen napkin, and bleached straw mat—are linked by a common color.

opposite below This ingenious pleated diamond-shaped napkin is perfect for creating unusual shapes and novel table decoration.

White on white conjures up many images, but most apt is a wedding or a grand banquet with the lavish attendant regalia of gleaming crystal, fine white bone china, and silver service.

left   If you have many guests, it is a good idea to fold the napkins the day before. This is an ideal job for children to want to join in the preparations.

right   A well-laid table is a visual pleasure; it not only looks inviting, but it makes guests feel welcome. Napkins are folded in half, then into three, and set in the center of each diner's plate (they may also be set on the left-hand side). They are shaken out as the diner is seated and spread over the lap. Small bunches of hand-picked roses add a personal touch to the occasion.

perfect day for a party

opposite This wonderful collection of French damask cotton and damask linen napkins with hand-embroidered monogrammes dates from between 1880 and 1920.

right These exquisite hand-embroidered napkins deserve a beautiful setting. Here they are teamed with a Victorian set of silverware with mother-of-pearl engraved handles.

below French 19th-century napkins are usually at least 28 to 30 inches or even a yard square. This size makes a sumptuous fold.

The monogram was a European bourgeosie invention—if your family did not have a coat-of-arms or a crest, you used your initials instead. Monogrammed napkins traditionally formed part of a young woman's dowry. If they were made before a betrothal, they carried the initial of her first name only. After a betrothal the initials of the couple were intertwined. The bride's collection of linen in her dowry, prepared by all the women in the household, was expected to last her a lifetime.

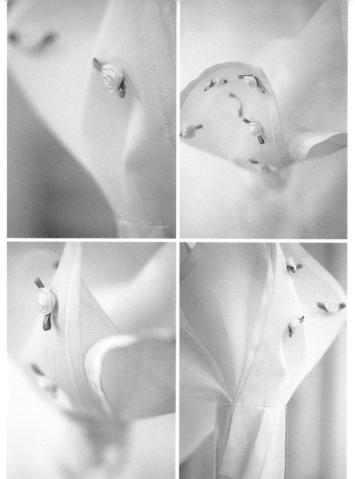

One way to add a little panache to an occasion (with the minimum of expenditure) is to either make or buy a set of fine cotton, organza, or organdy white napkins and stitch small roses or other decorations on one corner. Decorative satin and silk flowers may be purchased from napkins counters in most large department stores.

Spread the napkin out and lay upon it the pattern and amount of flowers you think will look most effective. Make a small pencil mark under each and then sew them in place. A haphazard pattern often works better; remember to keep an area of napkin free for use by the diner. White roses on white linen are ideal for weddings, christenings, and engagement parties. Another idea on the same white-on-white theme is to place a single fresh white rose on a folded white napkin.

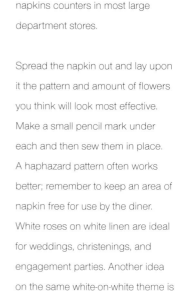

this page A fine white napkin sewn with satin flowers is decoratively fanned out in a champagne glass— perfect for a reception.

checks & stripes

Simple, rustic table linen always evokes appetizing thoughts of simple country fare, home-baked bread, and eating alfresco. Checks coordinate perfectly with stripes—put a striped placemat with a checked napkin and alternate each setting. The choice of bold colors can enliven the most basic setting.

Gingham check comes in a plethora of colors and with a couple of napkins in each, an impressive set can be quickly created. This graphic pattern is as old and familiar as the hills and can be used to great advantage to create an informal and inviting lunch. Checked napkins are available ready made and if you can sew, then the choice of cottons from madras to taffeta is limitless.

this page Sharp design and bright colors: checks and stripes are always fun.
right A jamboree of napkin parcels are placed in a basket for guests at an outdoor buffet.

Checks in different color combinations and styles can be mixed together arbitrarily to create an eclectic vibrant mix that is perfect for parties or casual entertaining. To avoid visual indigestion, keep plates and tablecloths plain, preferably white, if you are aiming for a jumbled effect. Or, if you prefer a slightly more controlled effect, they can be effectively linked together by a common theme. Group napkins by design, a tiny gingham check, for example, or maintain a single color theme.

Checked napkins are particularly suitable for family use as they withstand wear and tear, and they can be used for several days without obvious signs of use—keeping them in personal rings means they do not get muddled.

above and right A collection of rustic check cotton napkins looks effective decorated with a fringe. In the Middle Ages napkins with embroidery and fringes were reserved for the host and guest of honor.

opposite A faded 25-year-old French cotton-check napkin has a nostalgic charm.

opposite Napkins can add a touch of humor as well as being perfectly functional. These are all made from men's cotton shirting stripes, a soft fabric that is ideal for napkins. Striped shirting blues in a variety of stripe thicknesses suit white china dishes and coordinate well with a blue tablecloth.

below A brand-new set of cheerful fringed napkins is still tied with string. The color tones perfectly with bone-handled flatware.

right A crisp royal blue checked napkin is the perfect companion for everyday settings.

When you mix stripes together, the whole table setting should be considered. If there are too many lines in different directions, it could prove distracting or uncomfortable for some guests. Therefore, as with checks, plain colored table linen is invaluable. Combine blue-and-white stripes with a plain blue tablecloth to highlight the graphic nature of the design. Checks and stripes do not sit easily with other types of pattern, so it is always wise to make sure there is some calm expanse of table, be it on the china or the tabletop, to avoid overwhelming the food itself, which is, of course, the important thing!

plaid en plein air

Check is the traditional picnic pattern and always sets the mood. Picnics can be immense fun— there are so many innovative lightweight plastic containers available that are perfect for informal and lively outdoor eating. Mix and match checked napkins or ask your guests to bring their own.

opposite A tablecloth strewn across the grass holds an irrisistible spread. **right and above** Napkins can serve a multitude of purposes at a picnic.

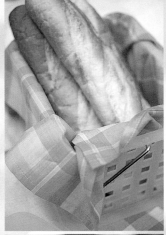

opposite Napkins tend to blow away if it is breezy, but there are several ways of anchoring them. Here a small decorative peg from South America clips a napkin to the edge of the cloth, but ordinary clothespins would work just as well. Flatware is an obvious anchor, or try smooth pebbles and shells, twigs, or fallen nuts (if the time of year is right).

this page Brightly colored plastic or tin utensils are available from hardware stores at very reasonable prices. The stacked baskets used for serving Chinese food are useful, too: look in Chinese supermarkets.

teatime treats

This sweet pink and blue table mat and napkin is a perfect breakfast setting for a house guest. It can equally be used as the setting for a morning tray. Children love to have a personal household item that is used on birthdays, Easter, or special occasions, and this could be ideal.

one You will need blue and pink gingham, solid blue and pink cotton, and matching blue and pink ready-made bias binding. Cut the plain cotton into a rectangular shape. Cut four strips from the gingham, each slightly longer than the sides of the rectangle, and slightly more than twice the width you want for the finished border.

two Place one short and one long strip right sides together and sew to a point. Trim the excess fabric. Miter all the strips together this way to form a frame.

three Turn the complete border right side out, press, and insert the rectangle into it. Sew the border in place.

. . . and for bias border Cut a large square from gingham, and fold and pin the bias binding all around the edge. Sew in place, turning the ends of the binding under for a neat finish.

lift flap ▶

Taffeta napkins in unusual color combinations give an edge to an informal supper party. If used merely for decoration, they can be left beneath the soup plate and another napkin provided by the host—who will then remove them completely when the main course is served.

above An exquisite small cake is wrapped in a capacious checked napkin to protect fingers and clothes.

right A jaunty rustic check is an ideal napkin for wrapping a casual lunch on the run.

fusion

The cosmopolitan climate we enjoy offers an exciting and colorful abundance of textiles and tableware from all over the world. Our diet now encompasses dishes not only from Europe, and the Middle and Far East, but from most parts of the globe. Eastern influences, particularly Thai and Japanese, have enriched our cuisine.

This fusion of tastes has influenced our tableware as receptacles and accessories for different purposes are required. Beautiful tea sets from Japan; lacquered ware and fine pots from Vietnam, raw silk napkins and bowls from China; porcelain spoons; Indian metalware—all can be easily obtained or collected on travels in order to create an inspired and unusual table setting.

left and below As we experiment with new recipes, so the style of our tableware and utensils follows suit.

Napkins are not traditionally used in Eastern cultures. Instead, it has long been the custom to offer guests small hot damp towels at the end of a meal, with which they can wipe their mouth and clean their hands—this practice can be witnessed in the Western world in Chinese and Indian restaurants.

The use of Eastern-style napkins in other cultures has been a result of crossfertilization. Eastern cuisines were influenced by Western dining styles, and the practice of using napkins became more common. Napkins using fabrics and decorative syles typical of the native culture and artistic heritage began to be produced and in turn have been introduced onto Western dining tables.

Many contemporary oriental napkins are quite unusual. They are often fashioned from raw silks or pigment-dyed linens which, when combined with the distinctive pottery glazes of the East, create a soft and muted palette of color and texture that can happily find a place in any style of table decoration.

opposite and right Cultures clash with harmonious results: black Korean dishes, a rice bowl from Vietnam, a brown napkin and wooden napkin ring from Europe, and decorated wooden chopsticks from Japan sit on a Japanese raw silk placemat. Although individual items do not belong to a particular set, the color theme is complementary, and chopsticks always create a good focal point by straddling a bowl or plate.

left and below A bamboo design on the serving plates echoes the bamboo coasters. The handleless china mugs for tea are cupped in the hand. Japanese chopsticks differ from Chinese ones in having pointed rather than blunt ends.

opposite Although napkins are not a traditional part of Japanese dining culture, the heavy linen ones used here have a suitably Eastern feel.

Japanese meal

Japanese tables are traditionally low on the floor. You can create the whole Japanese dining experience by covering a coffee table or solid wooden palette with a large piece of linen and laying cushions or woven *tatami* mats on the floor for your guests to sit on. A selection of plates, bowls, cups, lacquer boxes, coasters, and napkins can easily be acquired from oriental supermarkets.

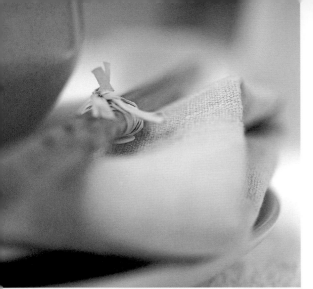

Bowls for holding communal food and for rice are common in Eastern cultures, and there must always be a rice bowl at each place setting. The bowls are useful for resting chopsticks before the meal if you do not have chopstick rests. A delicate napkin can be collapsed lengthwise into the center, which is particularly effective with contrasting colors of bowl and napkin. It is traditional for the host to serve the rice into bowls and etiquette dictates that guests should receive the bowl with both hands. Strictly speaking, you should not begin to eat until you have been served with rice.

Many styles of chopsticks are marketed, such as chased silver handles with ebony sticks, colored lacquers, colorful plastics, or disposable wood, which are available at oriental supermarkets but not ecologically sound as trees must be chopped down to make them.

left The raw silk handwoven undercloth is from a village in Vietnam where the industry has recently been revived. The wooden chopsticks are hand carved, decorated in Japan, and tied with raffia to indicate this pair belongs to its place setting. It is not good manners to place chopsticks upright.
right Celadon as a color for tableware has, until the recent vogue, been seldom used for dining in Western culture. It was prized for over a millennium in the East by collectors, scholars, and the court. Shades of celadon vary from very pale, scarcely discernible icy blues, to the jade color seen here. The color is calming, and enhanced by soft natural shades and textures.

opposite Create your own tea ceremony with well-chosen accessories. The intricate fish- and wave-patterned cloth is handwoven in Japan, and the tableau is set off by a branch of white blossom. **right** A cup and teapot sit on a bamboo mat. **below** Tea cakes—made from compressed tea leaves—are wrapped in individual portions.

While Eastern culture has many traditions laid down about the style and manner of eating, on no other occasion are there so many rules as at the *cha-no-yu*, or Japanese tea ceremony. It is like a spiritual ritual. The manner in which tea is served is defined according to the tenets of Zen Buddhism, and the ceremony symbolizes aesthetic simplicity through the elimination of the unnecessary.

The most formal ceremony can take up to four hours, and two types of green tea are served. Following a prescribed pattern, the host will ceremoniously lay out the cup and set the kettle to boil. Often the host will change his clothes, the room will be adorned

with flowers, and guests are expected to contemplate and praise the table setting, the tea canister, the glazed pottery, and every object associated with the occasion. Although it is not really practical in today's busy lifestyles to devote so much time to the basic function of drinking tea, it can be fun to invite a few friends over and approximate the experience by selecting Japanese tableware, such as beautiful porcelain bowls and cups, and napkins made from silk and embroidered or printed linen.

above A porcelain bowl and spoon sit on an embroidered silk placemat.

right A traditional bamboo design covers a Japanese cup.

oppposite, clockwise from top left This satin placemat is made from Chinese fabric. Handmade in Japan, this raw silk coaster is decorated with a diamond pattern in two colors. A hand-blocked cotton Indian napkin complements a bowl of cardamom seeds, which are used to freshen the breath. A soft linen napkin has a soft velvet border.

left, below, right, and opposite The strong shapes and graphic appearance of traditional Japanese sushi demands a similarly sharp line in the table decoration. Choose napkins in strong shades of naturally dyed linen and keep embellishments to an absolute minimum.

oriental dining

A Japanese meal is said to be an aesthetic experience. The food is always exquisitely prepared in bite-sized morsels of varying shapes, sometimes wrapped in a ribbon of seaweed. Japanese dining demands a particular treatment in keeping with the clean lines of the food. Natural weaves and simple decoration such as small beads are all that are needed. Embroidered wool in regular patterns such as blocked rectangles or a border of simple running stitch have the right geometric feel.

Napkin rings should be kept similarly simple in design to complement the graphic edge. Roll napkins with a pair of chopsticks in a horn or bone napkin ring, or fold them into neat shapes to echo the square design of a sushi plate or traditional lacquer box.

lift flap ▶

The traditional weaving, sewing, and embroidery of the East has been adapted with great effect to provide placemats and coasters for Western tables, although as the world grows smaller and global trade facilitated, table settings are beginning to fuse in their function. There is a pleasing simplicity of form in many Eastern crafts and a tactile appeal in tea cups and bowls that are held in the hand and not by handles.

column far left Silk cloth woven in two bright colors is folded as a cushion under a red lacquered Vietnamese dish and set with silver engraved chopsticks.

left The Indian craft of hand-embroidered mirror work is innovatively adapted as subtle decoration on a black organdy napkin. This creates a stylish combination with the gold underplate and black chopsticks threaded through the highly lacquered napkin ring.

right This vibrant oriental turquoise silk cloth and multi-lacquered cup and saucer set is from Vietnam. Spring blossoms float in green Japanese tea.

floral

Napkins with flower designs are a favorite theme, from full-blown chintzy prints to simple cotton with a flower embroidered in one corner. For occasions such as engagements, weddings, or a young girl's party, napkins can be adorned with silk flowers.

Continuing the theme, fresh flowers are a fragrant and romantic addition to a table, inside or outdoors. Roses, rose petals, daisies, buttercups, garden flowers, and herbs will enhance any setting and can be strewn or placed in low vases or baskets.

left   Flowers provide the inspiration for a range of napkins.
below   Strawberry sherbet is set off by a pretty print.

this page Embroidered daisies on a pure white linen napkin gives a light springtime touch to a luncheon table setting.

above A red flower lifts the all-white theme to lend a splash of color.

below White-on-white delicate floral embroidery and appliqué on fine linen is the perfect partner for bone china at a formal tea.

right A lace-edged embroidered handkerchief doubles as a napkin in a delicate hand-painted Limoges cup.

Embroidered napkins and tablecloths were very popular in Victorian and Belle Epoque times. Pretty pieces—often with freehand embroidered cottage garden scenes filled with character—are still plentiful in country antique fairs, second-hand bric-à-brac stores, and flea markets.

opposite, clockwise from top left A faded floral print complements the geometric pattern on the tableware. A contemporary floral design is chosen to lift the clean graphic lines of a glass and plate. A pink floral napkin enhances the colors and pastimes of summer. Colorful Japanese handkerchiefs are ideal as small cocktail napkins.

this page Soft flowers on a napkin used for a dessert of fresh fruit evoke Impressionist paintings and enhance the pleasure of al fresco eating.

this page Vibrant colors add fun and zest to table settings on party occasions.

It is not always possible to find the perfect color or texture of napkin to suit the occasion or the setting. But napkins are quite simple to make, and for special parties remnants of chiffon or organza are quite easy to find. The more delicate fabrics usually need to be hemmed by hand. The notions counters of large stores offer a wonderful selection of bindings, braids, sew-on motifs, beads, ribbons, and trinkets that can be used to decorate and customize your napkins.

above Embroidered ribbon daisy motifs are stitched on delicate white organza for a light and ethereal effect—perfect for a wedding or christening.

left Sew rich burgundy roses onto a chiffon napkin and your table decorations will become fashion accessories to create a decadent partner for chocolate cake!

morning coffee

Designer Christian Lacroix says, "Fashion doesn't just mean clothes, it means a whole lifestyle." This setting exemplifies the trend for style in homeware created by some of the world's leading fashion designers.

Here, Lacroix combines his taste for the unusual and his inimitable talent for blending colors. The result is a fanciful balance between the classic and contemporary. Although the occasion might be quite formal, it can be fun to introduce color, wit, and a sense of drama.

this page and opposite Haute couture-inspired coffee pot set and table linen from Parisian designer Christian Lacroix bring a touch of theater to the table.

folding napkins

Folded napkins look chic on formal occasions and can also be immense fun at a party. There are many different shapes to experiment with— some more difficult to master than others. It is not essential that folds match, and it can look very effective to set the table with several different examples or perhaps two styles alternating.

tuxedo

The "tuxedo" is stylish and very easy to master. It is particularly useful for buffets at which guests will receive their silverware and napkin together, and for elegant picnics or *fêtes champêtres* where

the flatware provides an anchor for the table linen. A placecard or sweet herbs may also be tucked into one of the folds for a personal touch. This fold works best on a large plain white napkin that is perfectly square. For best results and a really crisp edge, press and spray starch the napkins before you begin.

one Fold the napkin in half and then in half again to form a square a quarter of the size of the open napkin. (If you are going to use the folded napkin to hold flatware, check at this point that the handles are not too long for the napkin; if they are you will have to use larger napkins.) With the open corners positioned at the top left, fold the top layer back over the opposite corner so it forms a triangle. **two** Fold back each

of the next two layers in turn. Do not fold them back all the way—instead tuck the corner of each under the previous fold to form a rippled effect. When you are happy with the proportions, press the folds flat with your thumb. **three** Fold the right-hand third of the napkin to the back, including all folded layers. To finish, fold the left-hand third under and then slide your flatware or other decoration into the fold.

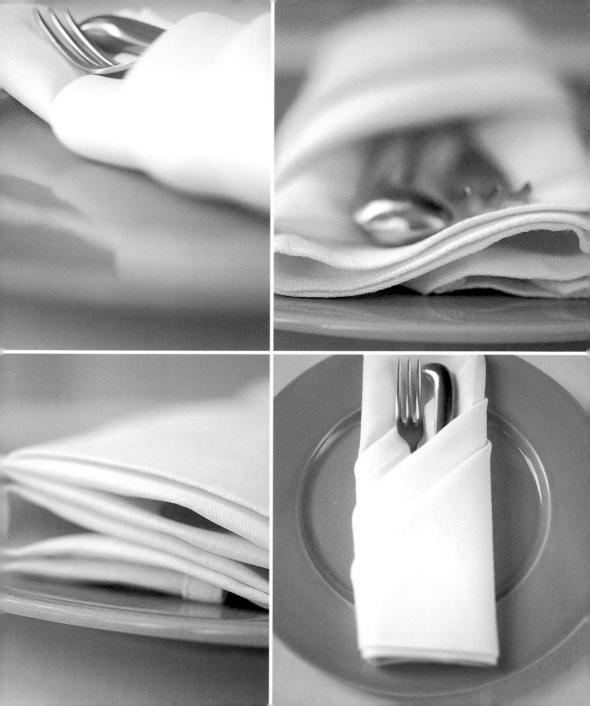

envelope

A simple fold for a light lunch or informal supper, the "envelope" does not require a starched napkin, and it is best fashioned from soft supple fabrics that will drape well. Solid as well as striped or check napkins are most suitable for this fold—stripes when folded often create their own pleasing geometric pattern.

one Fold the napkin in half to form a large rectangle, with a short end nearest you. To make the flap of the envelope, form a point at the top end of the

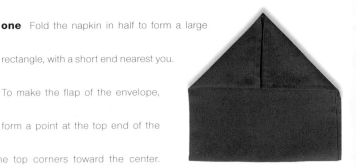

rectangle by folding down each of the top corners toward the center. Make sure the edges meet neatly. **two** Fold the lower half of the rectangle up to completely cover the pointed top half. For the second flap, fold down the corners of the top layer to meet in the same way as before to form another point over the top of the first one. **three** Fold the top pointed layer down so that the tip of the point reaches just below the bottom edge. Make a crease along the fold with your thumb. Fold down the second pointed flap over the first; do not crease this fold but leave it soft. Place the second flap slightly higher than the lower one so the double layer of flaps is clearly visible.

diamond

An excellent choice for a sit-down

occasion of four or more guests, this fold

can be stacked in advance. Napkins do

not have to be starched, but choose a fabric that holds a crease. The

"diamond" center is the perfect place for a placecard or bouquet of herbs.

one First make a narrrow rectangular strip by

folding the bottom third of the napkin up and

then the top third down to cover the lower

third. Holding the center point of the top edge

with your finger, fold the left half of the restangular strip diagonally downward.

two Turn the napkin over from left to right so the folded end is now underneath. Fold

one corner of this lower flap in and then repeat with the other corner so that the flap forms a triangular point.

three Place your finger at the midpoint of the left-hand diagonal edge of the napkin. With your other hand,

fold the triangular flap diagonally right and upward, so the lower

point now forms the right-hand corner of the diamond. To

finish, fold the right-hand half of the strip under so the diamond

sits neatly on a square border. Crease the fold with your thumb.

water lily

One of the best-known folds, and a favorite with children who

make it from paper to createye a guessing game, the "waterlily" is

equally suitable for both formal and

informal occasions. If you want a

flat, open lily, use napkins made of soft, unstarched fabric; a crisper

'abric will create sharper edges and a taller, bowl-like shape.

one To find the exact center of the napkin fold it in half to form a

rectangle and crease the fold with your thumb. Open out and repeat the fold the

other way. The point at which the folds meet is the center.

Fold each of the corners of the napkin in so they meet

at the centre to form a square. **two** Fold one corner in again,

making sure it is exactly in the center. **three** Fold the other three corners into the

center to form a smaller square. **four** Carefully lift the napkin and turn it over from left to right, keeping all of the

folded corners tucked underneath. Fold one of the corners into the center. **five** Fold each of the other three corners

into the center so that you once again form a square. **six** Holding the points

at the center with your fingers, gently pull out the flap from under one of the

corners. Pull out each of the other corners to form the petals of the waterlily.

lift flap ▶

placecard holder

This is a more complex fold that is worth the practice. The card holder is ideal for large dinner

parties where placecards are necessary. This fold needs a large napkin, heavily starched to hold

the tight rolls required, and is suited to white, cream, or solid colors.

one First make a narrrow rectangular strip by folding the bottom third of the

napkin up and then the top third down over the

lower third. Holding the center point of the bottom

edge with your finger, fold the left half of the strip

diagonally upward, and then the right half. Turn the

napkin over from top to bottom so that the point is now at the top. **two** Roll one

of the lower flaps up tightly until it meets the fold. Anchor it in place with

something heavy and then roll up the other flap. **three** Turn the

napkin over from top to bottom so that the point is now at

the bottom once more and the two rolls are at

the top. Fold the left-hand side down toward the bottom point, so the roll

lines up with the central vertical fold. Fold the right-hand side down to the bottom

point so the two rolls line up alongside one another. Slide your placecard between the

two rolls. The name should be written high enough on the card to be instantly visible.

fan

The "fan" is a favorite of many restaurants and is

easy to make. It requires heavy damask cotton or linen

napkins to make the most of the pleated effect. The

rear "tail" serves to anchor the fan on the plate.

one Starching is essential for this fold or the fan will not stand

upright. Spray starch the entire napkin before you start, and then

fold the napkin in half to form a rectangle. To create the fan

effect, start to pleat from one of the short ends of the rectangle in even,

equal-sized folds; each fold should be approximately 1 inch (2.5 cm)

wide. Starch and iron each crease as you fold so that the pleats are stiff

enough to stand upright like an accordion when the napkin is flat.

Continue in this way until half the rectangle is pleated in sharp folds. **two** Fold the napkin in half lengthwise.

The pleats should be on the outside of the fold, so that they can fan out, and the open edge

of the napkin should be at the top. **three** Fold the unpleated portion

of the napkin diagonally downward to prevent the pleats at the top of

the fan from opening up. Fold this strip under the bottom edge to form

the supporting tail. Finally, allow the pleats to fan out to their full extent.

french lily

An advanced, lofty fold, the "French lily" can create quite a spectacular effect as it sits extremely high upon the plate. It suits an extravagant, candlelit baroque occasion.

one Press and spray starch the napkin, then fold it in half diagonally to form a triangle. With the folded edge of the triangle nearest you, fold one corner of the triangle up to the top point. Fold the other corner up to meet it exactly so that you form a square with one corner pointing down, with a vertical seam where the two edges meet.

two Fold the bottom corner of the square up and then fold it back down on itself so that the tip of the corner sits exactly on the bottom edge and the vertical seams are aligning. Crease the folds with your thumb. **three** Fold the left-hand corner inward, open it out by inserting your finger in it, and then press it flat to form a kite shape. Press the right-hand corner open in the same way. **four** Pick up the napkin, wrap the two corners around to the back, and tuck them into each other. The turned back corners will help to support the napkin and give it a strong tubular shape when it is standing upright. **five** Bend the two loose points down, and to secure them, tuck their tips into the turn-up at the bottom. Do not crease the fold; a soft curve will give a more pleasing effect. Finally, fold down the front layer of the top point.

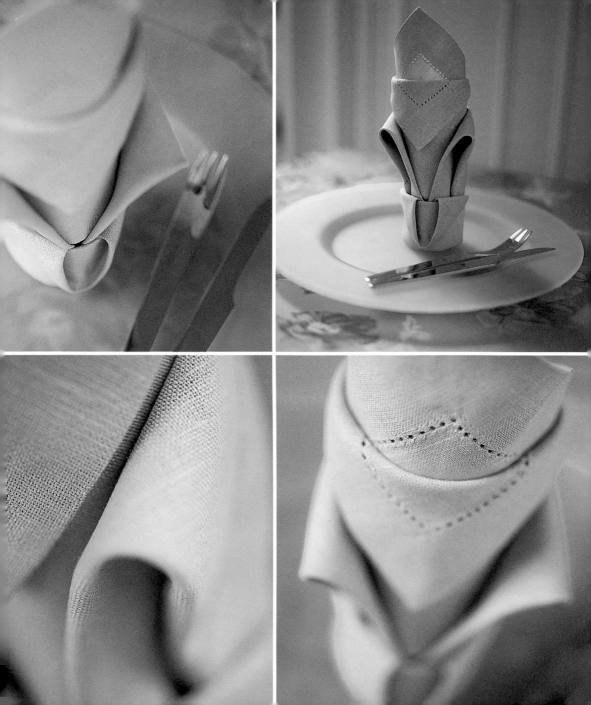

guard of honor

Folding napkins into tall shapes is an ingenious way of adding a vertical dimension to a table arrangement. To achieve a crisp finish it is vital that you use cotton or linen napkins and that you starch them well before you start; otherwise, they will not be stiff enough to stand upright.

one The larger the napkin you use, the taller your finished design will be. First fold the napkin in half to form a rectangle. Crease the fold with your thumb and then open the napkin out again so that it is flat. Fold the top and bottom halves of the napkin into the middle so that the edges meet at the creased center line. Holding the two edges together at the center point of the napkin with your fingers, fold back each corner in turn at an angle to form a flat windmill shape. **two** Starting at one of the short ends, roll up the napkin tightly until you reach the

central point. Place something heavy on the rolled side to keep it in place or it may spring back. **three** Roll the second half tightly into the center to meet the other roll. Pick up the napkin and bend the rolled napkin so the ends slot through each other. Place a knife and fork though the base of the napkin to anchor it in place and to prevent the ends from springing outward.

the boat and robin hood

Similar in construction, the "boat" and "Robin Hood" are fun, effective folds that can add wit to the occasion. Strong plain colors are best to show off their construction. Both are large folds, so they will need to sit on dinner plates rather than take up space on the table.

one First press and starch the napkin. Fold the napkin in half and then in half again to form a square a quarter of the size of the open napkin. Fold this square in half diagonally to form a triangle. Position the napkin with the point of the triangle at the top, with the loose corners rather than the folded corners uppermost. **two** Holding the topmost point, fold both two sides downward, so the corners lie below the folded edge of the napkin. **three** Turn the napkin over from left to right. Fold one of the lower points up over the folded line. Repeat with the other fold so you have a tall triangular shape. **four** Fold both sides together with the folds on the inside and then turn the napkin over so it sits on the base formed by the bulky tucks. To form the sails for the finished boat, pull each of the loose points up in graduated amounts.

. . . or to create the Robin Hood Proceed as for the first two steps above. Holding the top point with one hand, pull the top inner flap under the folds so it extends below the lower edge. Repeat with the other flaps in graduated amounts. Fold the napkin in half and tuck the folds at the back to secure.

lift flap ▶

There are many ways to embellish napkins. Traditional white napkins can be tied with colored ribbons to encourage a party mood, fresh flowers can be tucked into the family's napkin rings on a summer's evening, or old napkins can be given new life with the addition of braids or buttons.

decorating napkins

opposite, clockwise from top left A coiled satin rope-braid napkin ring gives textural interest and adds to the contemporary use of materials in this quiet setting. Napkin rings evocative of costume jewelry add glamour and extravagance to a party night. An engagement ring makes a charming napkin clasp for a romantic anniversary dinner for two. Stones encased in wire, reminiscent of modern sculptural jewelry, are innovatively used as napkin rings on smart accordion-pleated napkins. Long wooden beads are tied onto narrow strips of leather and used as a simple napkin tie. Jazzily patterned glass beads are threaded in the same way for a complementary setting at the same occasion.
below left and right Wire-edged ribbons are easy to manipulate into napkin rings because they hold their shape. Choose one of the many designs available featuring motifs for parties with a particular theme. These teddy bear motif ribbons, matched with simple white napkins dotted with blue, are fun for a children's party, and they can be taken home as a gift afterward.

Modern table settings have traveled a long way from the formality of the traditional setting, with their prescribed rules and strict adherence to etiquette. However, even in the court at Versailles, there was always a sense of theater and wit at the table settings on special occasions and at banquets, such as the intricate ways in which napkins were folded to represent birds, flowers, and fruit, and we can take our cue from this treatment for our own more humble celebrations.

Today we see many of our fashion designers moving into the homeware arena, bringing with them their creativity and ability to mix colors, textures, and glamour. We now have an enormous variety of ways in which we can decorate and embellish our table settings. Inexpensive jewelry can be used for the table; napkins may be tied with bracelets, necklaces wound round and round, beads threaded onto ribbon or leather; and notions-counter trimmings can create unusual ties.

decorating napkins

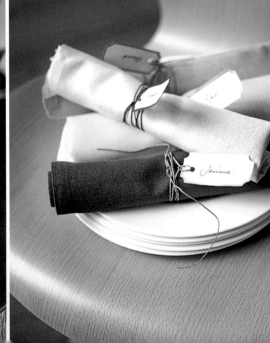

opposite above Narrow satin ribbons, threaded through holes punched through small colored envelopes, are used to tie rolled-up napkins. A personal message or announcement can be inserted in the envelope.

opposite below left Different napkins—in checks, stripes, or solids and tied with satin ribbons—create a jolly and informal atmosphere.

opposite below right Luggage tags attached with fine string are a novel way to decorate napkins – good for a party before a trip overseas.

this page Edible pastries are a fun idea. Cut them with cookie cutters, and remember to make a hole for ribbon. Initials can also be added before baking.

natural beauty

Take advantage of what nature has to offer in every season. Snip a small cluster of roses or various leaves from the shrubbery, keep nuts from the autumn harvest, or if you do not have a yard use small fruits or fresh herbs from the supermarket. Beachcombing provides a cornucopia of goodies such as shells, sea-smoothed pebbles, and small unusual shapes of driftwood.

this page and opposite Natural decorations are simple and most effective: try vine leaves, individual flowers, shells, fresh herbs, a pear, hazel nuts, or a daisy chain.

Shells and artefacts made from tiny to large shells are visually and texturally ideal for use as table decoration. Once cleaned, they have myriad uses, from individual receptacles for salt and pepper, oyster shells used as candle holders or as a plate for scallop dishes or garnishes, to napkin rings and embellishments. Even something as simple as a selection of tiny shells sprinkled across the table make a pretty and unassuming table decoration.

Rolled-up name tags made from creamy parchment or vellum can be placed inside larger individual shells and placed on a napkin. Mother-of-pearl and the interior of abalone shell add to the appeal of an all-white setting and can also be put to imaginative uses.

left above and below The oval shape of a conch shell has been utilized to form a perfect napkin ring. The ends have been sawn off and sanded smooth so a napkin can be threaded through, and the edges curve around to form a natural clasp. The *fruits de mer* theme is maintained with a flat plate fashioned from natural shell.

opposite page Tiny mother-of-pearl buttons backed with tortoiseshell have been sewn onto the corner of a marine blue napkin. When adding decorations to napkins, remember to confine the decorations to one corner only, so the napkin can still serve its purpose. An unusual spoon fashioned from several different seashells and a pearly white plate create an unusual setting and a witty offering for a seafood supper.

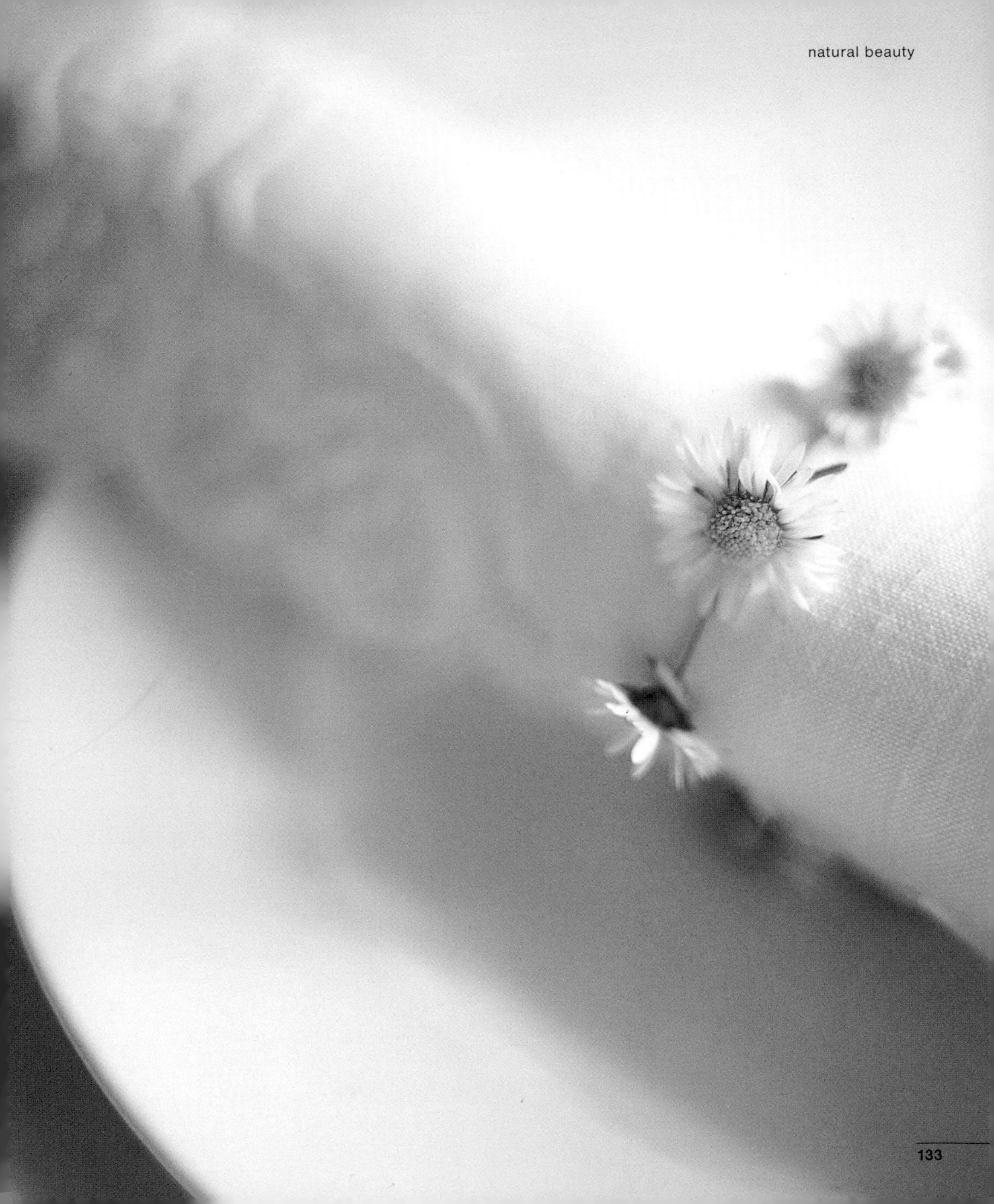

decorative edgings

Napkins are simple to make. It is also fun to make a mix-and-match set in complementary colors. Here a traditional trim and simple embroidery stitch are given a modern feel with bright colors. The graphic outline of rickrack creates a contemporary country style, while blanket stitch in a contrasting shade of silk thread is a very effective finish. Used on napkins and on table mats, they make a colorful set that can be expanded to include as many place settings as necessary.

one You will need large squares of thin cotton or linen in different colors, rickrack, and silk embroidery floss Hem around all four sides and machine stitch the rickrack around the edge to form a border. **two** For the banket-stitched napkins, turn a double hem all around a square of fabric, folding the corners in first to make a neat miter. Press the hem in place and then use blanket stitch to hold it in place. To form the stitch, sew at a right angle to the hem and pull the needle through the loop of thread to hold it in place.

embroidered checks

Cross stitch is one of the first embroidery stitches that we teach children and is particularly appealing on checked fabric or gingham. A basic checked napkin can be made into something a bit more special by the addition of a little simple embroidery. Here white silk thread is embroidered onto jolly red and white checked French linen. Just a couple of rows of checks are highlighted in a central square pattern.

one Select a napkin with a small checked pattern; if you try to cross stitch a large square, the stitches will be too long and will snag too easily. Thread your needle with two strands of embroidery floss. **two** Decide which rows you want to sew and then work around the first row, making a basic cross stitch by sewing each square from corner to corner. Work around the second row in the same way. A cross stitch is made into a star by stitching another cross onto the original. Go back over the rows you have sewn, adding another cross from side to side of each square.

opposite The traditional red and white bandana favored by cowboys doubles as a napkin to wrap bread at a picnic.

below Two checked napkins wrapped around ice cream cones add to the fun of a children's summer party, and can later be used to mop up the inevitable meltdown.

above top left For a jaunty note, tie a floral napkin around the handle of a mug rather than folding it.

above below left A crisply starched napkin is placed inside a bread basket to gather crumbs. It can also be folded over to keep the brioches warm.

above A generous damask napkin is tied around a glass of mint tea so it can be comfortably picked up and the tea drunk while it is still hot.

left Wrap a small napkin around French bread to keep fingers clean.

japanese present

Many hosts like to present a small token to their guests. An effective way to do this is to wrap a small

gift in a box in a table napkin, as the Japanese do. This may be served at the beginning of the

evening or brought in, already tied up, before the dessert course, depending on the occasion.

one   You will need a large napkin

to wrap generously around a box.

If you wish the corners to remain pert,

the napkin should be starched or

made of a stiff fabric such as taffeta.

Lay the box at an angle to the corners.

two   Pick up two opposite corners and bring them together above the box. Roll them down and fold them

over the top of the box.   **three**   Fold in the excess fabric on each of the long ends to form narrow strips.

four Carefully pick up the wrapped

box and turn it over. Tie up the two

ends. The box will now be upside

down, so be sure your gift is secure

within it. It will be the right way up

when your guest unwraps the napkin.

Napkins can be used to wrap individual gifts at each place setting that also add the finishing touch to the decoration of the table setting as a whole. Miniature pots of flowers are plentiful in spring and summer. Small-headed garden flowers such as lavender, pansies, daisies, pinks, violets, or patio roses are ideal.

Another idea is to pot fresh herbs such as basil and thyme, which can then be used as a garnish with the meal. Little pots of spearmint or lemon verbena are also useful to rub on the hands after a course where guests have eaten with their fingers. Fold the napkin into a triangle and tie it around the pot with a contrasting ribbon or cord. Your guests can simply untie the napkin for use before the meal.

opposite and right A small pot of blue flowers is enfolded into a dotted napkin, tied with braid, and placed on a blue plate dotted with white. The combination of spots, blue, and white are chosen for their freshness, informality, and rustic appeal.

flatware bag

This useful flatware bag holds a single place setting—ideal for travelling, picnics, or as a gift. Choose a napkin made from a sturdy fabric such as heavy cotton or linen, with ribbon or cotton braid for the tie.

one Fold up the lower part of the napkin and lay your flatware on top to make sure it fits. Pin the edges and between each piece of flatware to mark the pockets. Be generous with the space so the bag will roll up easily. **two** When you are happy with the spacing, baste the pocket seams and remove the pins.

three Machine stitch the seams, double-stitching the top of each seam to secure. Remove the basting. **four** Fold the

braid or ribbon in half and slipstitch the folded end to one edge of the napkin. Place your flatware in the pockets, fold over the top flap, and roll the bag from the edge without the tie. Wrap the tie around and knot loosely.

lift flap ►

napkin bag

This bag, fashioned from one large linen napkin, is the perfect envelope for a set of napkins.

Napkins invariably get parted from their companions, so this is the ideal container. It is simple to

make, and it is a pretty and practical addition to any linen closet.

one Choose as large a napkin as you can find, or the bag will not hold napkins of

any size. One with a decorative border is ideal, since the trim will become a feature

of the finished bag; this one has a drawn-

thread hem. Select a fastening to complement

the style of your napkin. A frog fastening made

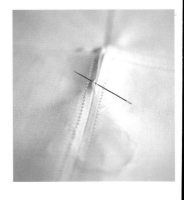

the style of your napkin. A frog fastening made

from braid is very decorative, and easy to attach, but you could also attach

two buttons and make a loop from thin cord. Fold each of the corners

into the center and press the folds. **two** Butt up the edges of the folded

corners rather than overlapping them, for a flat finish. Working on the

right side, slipstitch the edges together. Make tiny, neat stitches. **three**

Slipstitch the other edges together in the same way to form the envelope.

Sew the looped part of the fastening to the loose corner of the napkin that

will form the flap, working from the wrong side. Fold the flap over to work

out where the button should go. Sew it in place, working from the wrong side.

AUTHOR'S ACKNOWLEDGMENTS

First of all my thanks go to my assistant Robbie Spina for his commitment, support, and sense of style. Thank you to David Loftus for creating such evocative pictures and for his ability to continually discover a fresh approach; Tara Fisher for her enthusiasm and help with the deluge of ironing; Maya Babic for propping and styling; Beska Sorensen for her exquisite sewing and embroidery; designer Paul Tilby and my editor Sian Parkhouse; and to my agent Fiona Lindsay of Limelight.

I am also very grateful to the many people who graciously lent us their table linens, cutlery, china, and glassware. My thanks go particularly to Maryse and Bob Boxer for their generosity and encouragement; to Jane Sacchi for lending her monogrammed napkins; Le Jacquard Francais; The White House; Biche Tyler of Trade and Care; Wedgwood; Thomas Goode; and O'Reda.

I would like to thank my friends for their unique support and for letting me raid their linen and china cupboards. Thanks to Sylvia Knights for the silver cutlery; to Jo Zito for the use of his apartment; a huge thank you and hugs to Madgie and Bertie Varnham for looking after me while I wrote the text. An especial thank you to Douglas for that very welcome encouragement and support and to my daughter Emily for her constant vigilance, care and support too—thank you Ems.
MC

SUPPLIERS

Napkins

Ikea
To obtain catalog, write:
Ikea Catalog Department
185 Discovery Drive
Colmar, PA 18915

Calvin Klein Home
Flagship store:
654 Madison Avenue
New York, NY 10022
212-292-9000
800-294-7978 for a store
near you.

Crate and Barrel
650 Madison Avenue
New York, NY 10022
or
Crate and Barrel
P.O. Box 9059
Wheeling, IL 60090-9059
800-451-8217

Details at Home
1031 Lincoln Road
Miami Beach, FL 33139
305-531-1325

Gracious Home
1220 Third Avenue
New York, NY 10021
212-517-6300 or 800-338-7809

Pier 1 Imports
For a store in your area call
800-44PIER1 (800-447-4371)
*All kinds of stylish
accessories
for all the rooms in the
home. Nationwide locations.*

Pottery Barn
P.O. Box 7044
San Francisco, CA 94120-7044
800-588-6250
*Home accessories. Stores
Nationwide.*

Ralph Lauren Home Collection
1185 Sixth Avenue
New York, NY 10036
For a store in your area, call
800-377-POLO (800-377-7656)

Wolfman Gold & Good, Inc.
117 Mercer Street
New York, NY 10012
212-431-1888
*Furniture and accessories—
some old, some new, all
delightful.*

Fabrics

B & J Fabrics
263 West 40th Street
New York
NY 10018
212-354-8150

*Natural fiber fabrics
including velvets*

Calico Corners
203 Gale Lane
Kennett Square
PA 19348
800-213-6366
*Over 100 retail outlets that
discount top-quality fabrics*

Keepsake Quilting
Route 25B
P.O.Box 1618
Center Harbor
NH 03226-1618
800-865-9458
*Good selection of
lightweight cottons, plus
threads and notions*

Ian Mankin Fabrics
Available through
Coconut Company
129-31 Greene Street
New York
NY 10012
212-539-1840
*A complete line of cotton
fabrics in solids, stripes, and
checks*

Notions and Trims

Bell'occhio
8 Brady Street
San Francisco
CA 94103
415-864-4048
Vintage ribbons

Clothilde, Inc.
2 Sew Smart Way
Stevens Point
WI 54481-8031
800-772-2891
*Discounted notions and
trims*

Hyman Hendler & Sons
67 West 38th Street
New York
NY 10018
212-840-8393
*Fabulous selection of
ribbons*

M & J Trimmings
1008 Sixth Avenue
New York
NY 10018
212-391-9072
*A wide range of trimmings
including an exciting
collection of buttons*

Tinsel Trading Co.
47 West 38th Street
New York
NY 10018
212-730-1030
*Vintage to contemporary
trims, tassels, flowers,
fringes, buttons, cords, and
military trims*